Best Wishes!
Poetically Yours,
Sonali Shah
4-9-90

Touch of Class

A Collection of Poetry and Short Stories

by Sonali A. Shah

VANTAGE PRESS
New York / Los Angeles / Chicago

FIRST EDITION

All rights reserved, including the right of
reproduction in whole or in part in any form.

Copyright © 1989 by Sonali A. Shah

Published by Vantage Press, Inc.
516 West 34th Street, New York, New York 10001

Manufactured in the United States of America
ISBN: 0-533-084903

To all of those people who have touched my life with their own "touch of class" and especially to Mr. Clyde Wicker, my sixth grade teacher, who helped me to find my writing talent

Contents

Death and the Rose	1
Touch of Class	3
Our Two Worlds	4
A Night in New York City	5
Almost	7
Benjamin	8
Not for Me	9
Memories of January 11, 1987	10
He's Only a Dream	11
Gone Again	12
"Keep Trying"	13
Leather and Lace	14
Dear Danny	15
Could This Be Love?	16
Untold Secret	17
He's Only Human, Too!	18
Haiku	19
That One Mistake	20
Just When I Thought	21
One Night	22
The Library Study Desk	23
Remember Me	24
Afterword	25

Death and the Rose

"**I** LOVE YOU," he said, and with the rose beside him, he died.

Two years have passed since that awful day, but I still cannot seem to forget it. Sometimes I stay up at night wishing that it had been only a dream.

But even before I met him, my life had no meaning. My life was just ordinary and I had no will to live. I never went anywhere or did anything.

But then one day, two years ago, my friends forced me to go to the big school picnic.

It was the most wonderful time of my life, because that's where I met him, the first person who really paid any attention to me. Every time we met after that, he would give me a rose.

The first time we met he gave me a yellow rose. "It stands for friendship," he said.

The next time we met he gave me a pink rose, then he gave me a red rose. He explained what each color signified.

He told me that the pink rose stood for happiness and the red rose signified love. He also told me that one shouldn't give anyone white roses on Easter because they signified death.

From then on, life was perfect. We did everything together. We danced, we dreamed, we laughed, we talked, and we listened. I was in love. I just couldn't believe it.

Until that one dreadful day, I had thought my life was finally coming to order. But then one day, he told me something I had not known before, something I just could not believe. I did not want it to be true, but I knew it was. He said, "Good-bye."

Suddenly, my life began to fall apart. I couldn't take it anymore. I asked him for more details, but he gave me none. He did give me his hospital room number, however, but for days I could not bring myself to go visit him.

Things were happening too fast. I just needed more time to evaluate my feelings, but I knew I had no more time.

I finally went to see him. He smiled when I went in. I had brought him a red rose, and when he saw it, his face lit up again.

I could see that he was weak and tired, so I asked him not to speak but only to listen. I told him about the people at school who missed him and how much I loved him.

He just lay there quietly, listening to me. Then, before I knew it, he took my hand and said, "I love you." He took the rose I had given him, put it beside him, and died.

Looking back, I felt so frustrated. There was nothing I could do about his death. I tried many times to forget him, but I could not.

Time has passed now, and I stand by his grave thinking of all the good times we shared. Then I lay a rose by his grave and say, "I love you, too."

Touch of Class

I needed a reason for meaning in my life.
I needed something to pull me through
and then, out of nowhere, came you.
        And now . . .
I see love, I see you, I feel something
new in the air, since you brought a touch of
class into my life.
My life ahead was so unclear, the
future still unknown. I needed a
new light to see clearly, and then
you brought it to me.
        And now . . .
I see love, I see you, I feel something new
in the air, since you brought a touch
of class into my life.
Now I think I know you are the one
I will never let go. . . .
I see love, I see you, I feel something
new in the air, since you brought
a touch of class into my life.

Our Two Worlds*

You and me—
how can it be?
We come from different places. We each
have our own world. I know
I will never be your girl.
If only you weren't so nice, my
heart wouldn't take a chance
and pay the price.
Your world is so different—
wild, adventurous, and free—
while mine is just
innocent, naive, and has purity.
I really don't know where all
of this got its start;
It must have been in my heart.
One part of me wants to explore
the world you live in, while
the other knows I would never win.
Should I take a chance and step
into your world or should I
remain in my own—all alone?
I guess there's only one answer
to solve this rhyme—
                      Time!

*Picked as the "Golden Poem" by the World of Poetry Board of Directors in 1988.

A Night in New York City

As the warm bright sun began to set slowly, the coolness of the night air settled into the city. The street lights flashed on quickly, making every inch of the city visible. The stars danced a mischievous medley as the moon looked on. As I looked to my right, I saw the ferryboat coming back to shore, and within the boat, the passengers' faces were filled with awe. And as I looked to the distance, I could see why their faces were filled with such amazement. There she stood, the beautiful statue, one arm raised. She was facing to the east, her figure outlined by the pale moonlight. Even the water looked clear and calm. The pleasantness of the city seemed to come to an end when I looked to my left.

The busy streeets were filled with cars, noisily reaching their destination. I walked to a corner, and there I saw flashing neon lights telling me that I was in the heart of the city. There were beautiful faces being chased and green being exchanged into the wrong hands.

In the distance, I could hear a favorite Benjamin Orr song coming out of a twenty-four-hour coffee shop. I walked through the bustle only to hear the roar of a deafening subway. I stopped and looked up. I could see that every room was lit in the tall buildings. I kept walking into the darkness, passing a park. The trees had a beautiful silhouette against the sky, as they swayed in rhythm with the wind. Two figures walking hand in hand passed me. In the night, the silence spoke.

I walked over a small bridge, smelling the city for the first time. The air was chilly and the people that were out bundled closer together for warmth. I passed some gates slowly opening and closing with the rhythm of the wind. I paused, noticing he ground. The pebbles played up and down the wide paths; they were like small diamonds sparkling in the night. There were red and blue flashing lights in the distance; I knew right away what they were. They were common in this part of the city. As I came back to where I had started my walk, things were a little different.

Cars on the streets were less noisy, the street lights faded slowly, the moon began sinking into the clouds, the stars doing their mischievous dance were tiring slowly, and the coolness of the night air began to fade as it made room for the bright and warm sun to come up.

Almost

We came so close, but now I feel
that I'm slowly losing you.
Why does it have to end?
We had real love—were all those
things you said really true?

We had laughs, we had our fears,
we had dreams, and we had tears,
but we had love—almost.

Remember how we danced, hoping for a
little romance; we held each other
so tenderly. Why did you leave me?

The day you left—without saying sorry—
is all I remember, and now I see
it clearly—

That we had laughs, we had our
fears, we had dreams, and we had
tears, but we also had love—
Almost!

Benjamin

It started with the drive through
Heartbeat City. He sang so sweetly.
He always keeps me in harmony.
Oh, I don't know how all of this
got its start. Blonde hair, blue eyes,
and the key to open my heart.
Benjamin.

When he told me to stay the night,
I knew the moment was right.
And now I can't remember a time
I've ever been this happy.
All of this sounds pretty crazy.
It must be magic. Really!
Benjamin.

My heart leaped without looking,
and now you're all I see, you're
all I need.
Benjamin.

Not for Me

Why do I feel this way?
Why do I feel something toward you?
You are someone else's, I know
that's true. Yet I keep on loving you.
I guess it's love, because I feel so
very different around you. My heart
takes a leap at the sight of your
face, and I feel as if I must have
your warm embrace. Just the thought
of you near me is all it takes, at
least that's the impression my mind
makes. But I know now that we
were not meant to be, yet you
will always be very dear to me.
But it's time I learned that
I can't have you, that itself
will take time to get used to.

Memories of January 11, 1987

(Dedicated to Bernie Kosar, the Cleveland Browns vs. Denver Broncos.)

There I stood, alone, in the cold.
The day's events were only memories now—old.
　　Suddenly, a flashback. I relived it
all over again. I could feel it all
coming back. Is this ever going to end?
Everyone was depending on me. I had
to do something, anything, to make
them believe that their dreams
were slowly becoming a reality.
Everything was perfect! Fans came,
snow fell, and I was ready, more
ready than I've been before. Everything
was going our way—even the score.
But, then, things began to change.
I looked to my left, I looked to
my right, but there was no one in
sight. "What is happening?" I said.
But I knew that I was just being misled.
I looked up only to see that the
kick had been good and that was history.
Looking back, I knew there wasn't anything
I could do, because I was tired and
sad; but most of all, I was mad.
But this is not the end of me.
There's always next season—and
that's the reason. This is not
the end, only the beginning.

He's Only a Dream

Only in my dream does he hold me,
only in my dream do I hold him.
Only in my dream does he talk to me,
only in my dream do I talk to him.
Only in my dream he listens to me,
Only in my dream do I listen to him.
    I know he's only a dream.
Only in my dream does he walk beside me,
only in my dream do I walk beside him.
Only in my dream does he touch me,
only in my dream do I touch him.
    I know he's only a dream.
Only in my dream does he kiss me,
only in my dream do I kiss him.
Only in my dream he loves me,
only in my dream do I love him.
    I know he's only a dream.
Only in my dream is there love
and that love is a dream and
the dream is the only thing I have.

Gone Again

It happened one day—I wasn't expecting it. My mind was on something else. He had come into my life just like that—suddenly! I had seen him once before, for only minutes, then he was gone—never to return. So I thought, anyway. Time had passed and I had forgotten all about him. It wasn't until we met again that I knew only my mind had forgotten about him. I guess in my heart he was always there. He had come back again. Once again. Once more. Was he really there? He really was. But then it happened; suddenly, just like he had come, he was gone.

"Keep Trying"

All of my life I've waited,
but the things I have wanted
the most never came.
Even though I would try, the
rejections just made me cry.
Sure, I would dream, hoping
someday it would become a reality.
But that kind of joy was not meant
for me. Life sure is painful
when things are denied, and the
thing that hurts the most is my pride.
Still, I'll keep hoping that one
lucky day I'll find what I'm
looking for, but these feelings
will never go away. But no, I'll
never give up! A quitter is what I'm not.

"Keep trying," is what I've always
been taught.

Leather and Lace

He held me so close as the song
slowly came to an end. I knew now
that we were more than friends.

We walked outside, noticing the moon;
I wished the night wouldn't end so
soon. The stars shone so bright.
I knew the moment was right.

I could see it in his face. We were
as different as leather and lace, but
somehow, I didn't seem to care; we
did make a good pair.

He took me by the hand and said,
        "I love you," I knew then that
it was too good to be true. And
then, something I just couldn't
miss, he gave me a gentle kiss.

But then, as real as it seemed, I
awoke, only to find—that it
was only a dream.

Dear Danny

*(Dedicated in memory of my friend, Daniel Toomey.
May he rest in peace.)*

You were a friend to all; you were
always there when anyone felt like
they were going to fall.
You cared for even strangers, not
knowing the dangers.
Just those little things you did
really meant a lot.
You had a gift no one has got.
We were all there for you. Why didn't
you tell anyone you were so blue?
You thought you had no friend—but
we were all there, even till the end.
If only you had waited, then you would
have known that you were not hated.
Ten years ago, when we met, I knew
it was you, the one who would care;
and it was me, for all of your obnoxiousness,
I had to bear. But looking back at all
the years past, I couldn't believe we
were seniors at last. I'll always
cherish all of the memories, most of
them good, some bad; I'll try not to
be sad. Well, it's time I go. But before
I do, let me say that we all
loved you!

Could This Be Love?

WHAT MAKES ME so jumpy at your first sight? What makes me so afraid when I know I love you with all my might? Why does my heart panic when you're so near? Why do I have this fear? Why is there a constant battle between my heart and mind when I know that you are one of a kind? Why is everything all right when it's your smile I find?
Could this be love?

Untold Secret

When I first saw you, I never really paid much attention.
But then we met again.
You were different; fate must have brought us together.
    We laughed,
    We talked,
We shared our deepest thoughts.
Day after day you would enter my life—each time bringing more
    love. You were always there for me.
You were the only one who would listen and understand.
You were the only one I could tell
    My inner secrets,
    My darkest fears,
But then one day I found one secret, your secret, the one you
    never revealed to me, the one that said that we were never
    meant to be.
    You were already taken,
    But not by me!

He's Only Human, Too!
(Dedicated to David.)

People see the rough exterior part of him,
while I see the little boy still inside.

People see his life-style and feel they
don't belong, while I see his welcoming
world, where only I can hear his song.

People see his wild side and stay away,
while I see the little boy who just wants to play.

People see his *different* world and give me
disapproving looks each time I enter that world.
If only they knew how nicely he
treated me, like a real girl.

People fail to see his compassion and
overlook his sensitivity and caring; only
I see the person inside of him.

While people see this wild and rough
person, they forget one thing, the
thing I can see so clearly,
he's only human, too.

Haiku

1. He gently kissed me,
   and then the porch light flashed on.
   It was my parents.

2. The boy played outside;
   she suddenly came to greet him;
   now they are married.

3. The night air was cold;
   stars danced mischievously
   and the moon looked on.

4. The day you left me
   without saying you're sorry,
   but I still miss you.

That One Mistake

When we first met, friends was what
we were meant to be.
How did I know you were attracted to me?
Then one night a kiss or two was all,
but I knew my heart would fall.
And now I miss the way it used to be;
I miss those talks, just you and me.
It'll never really be the same. And all
because of that one mistake!
What went wrong? You stopped coming
around for a while. I really miss your smile.
Can we ever be friends,
like it was?
Or is this the end?
I miss the way it used to be,
I miss those talks, just you and me;
It'll never really be the same—all
because of that one mistake!

Just When I Thought

Just when I thought there was something
happening between us,
Just when I thought no one could touch me
the way he did,
Just when I thought the sad days were over,
Just when I thought there was magic once
again in my life,
Just when I thought he was the only one
for me,
Just when I thought I would never
have to be alone,
Just when I thought I was pretty,
Just when I thought things were fine,
Just when I thought I would never have to cry . . .
he said goodbye.

One Night

That one night seems like yesterday, not
far away. . . .
The room was lit, dim; I remember the setting
was perfect. And there I saw him.
He looked quite handsome. I wish I
could live that night all over again. For
after that, he would be gone, never to return.
I knew I had only one night.
I went over to him.
A quick hug was all he gave;
he held me close for only a short time.
Then slowly I let go.
I wish I could have held him forever.
But I knew time was up. . . .
I could still feel it, that night
reliving in my mind.
That one night seems like yesterday, not
far away.

The Library Study Desk

The Sunday breeze blew outside, while
I studied inside.

The quiet room was filled with studious
people, and in the calmness the silence
spoke.

Across the desk his feet slightly touched
mine as he sat down abruptly.
I looked up at him, only momentarily,
he glanced my way, he smiled.

The only view now was of his feet.
His tennis shoes were worn out;
I could tell he was athletic.
I remembered his face, so angelic.

I rose to the shelf as such,
when I felt his touch.
Oh, no! He needed the same book.

We came back; it was late. He asked me for
a date, but I left knowing that it
all started at the library study desk.

Remember Me

Remember that night. They played our song;
we danced until there was light.

And then remember our first kiss. You said
I was beautiful; I'll always cherish this.

But now it's time to let you go;
how I'm going to, I don't quite know.

It's so hard for me to say good-bye
without breaking down to cry.

Fate is so cruel; it was perfect what we had.
Please don't be sad.

This is the way it has to be; it's hard
because you are so important to me.

We did have it all, you know;
life was one big ball.

You're a part of my soul. I can never
forget you; you're true as gold.

And now I ask one thing before I leave,
please never forget me.

Afterword

My first thanks goes to God. Without him, nothing is possible.

Thanks to my family for their support through all of this; I know it's not easy living with me. I love you, Mom, Dad, and Shital.

Thanks, Mr. Wicker, for helping me find my creative writing talents; thanks for the inspiration and help.

Thanks to all of my friends for being who they are. You guys are the best!

Thanks to Lori and Karen for listening and being patient.

Thanks, Mike, for being you.

To Sherri, who affectionately calls me "Pie." Thanks for being there for me through thick and thin. I love you, sweetie!

And a special thanks to David. Thanks for seeing me as I really am. I will always love you.

Poetically yours,
Sonali